Thinking Fast and Slow: Revealed – The Surprising Truth about What Kahneman Means for Management

Andy Cor

DEDICATION

To all those aspiring managers who want to make the correct decision more often!

CONTENTS

ACKNOWLEDGMENTS

It is a privilege being able to write and to have this book published.
Thanks to Amazon and CreateSpace

i

Introduction

Management decisions make or break a company; the more frequently the wrong decision is made the faster the company is destroyed. You, as a manager know this. According to <u>Daniel Kahneman</u> (<u>Thinking Fast and Slow</u>), most people make the wrong decisions more often than the right ones! Daniel Kahneman's book is available from Amazon bookstores. Andy Cor sets out to help you as a manager to avoid making those wrong decisions.

In the book, Thinking Fast and Slow: Revealed – The Surprising Truth about What Kahneman Means for Management the key principles are briefly outlined and applied to a management scenario. In this way, you can obtain a quick grasp of the relevance of Professor Kahneman's principles to their management practices and can become a more effective manager with this knowledge and thus avoid making the wrong decisions. Note the examples are my own; the principles are those of Daniel Kahneman.

Daniel Kahneman

You as a manager are trained to think rationally and logically. You are expected to consider every move from as many angles as possible. You are expected to make rational decisions devoid of emotion and devoid of other irrelevant considerations. Sound decisions and good judgment are cornerstones of your management practice. The higher the stakes, the more your thinking has to disciplined thinking and the more care you need to take in considering your next actions.

However, as you and any seasoned manager know, it is impossible to make every decision rationally and unemotionally. Thinking is harder work and usually slower than making fast, intuitive decisions. Equally, it is challenging for staff to refrain from gossiping and it is difficult for staff and managers to resist indulging in making up stories in substitution for the facts.

This phenomenon of poor decision making and substitution of the facts is explained in a recent book by Daniel Kahneman, a Nobel Prize winning psychologist who discusses these thinking behaviors based on over 30 years of research. Professor Kahneman explains this phenomenon using two characters, System 1 and System 2. System 1 is characterized as the irrational, intuitive and often rapid thought processor. Conversely, System 2 is characterized as a slower, rational, calculating type of thought processor.

The differences between System 1 and System 2 are illustrated by Kahneman by using the example in an investment scenario. Using the example of Ford cars and investors, Kahneman relates how a manager invested in Ford stocks because it was easier for that manager to answer the question of whether or not he liked the car rather than answering the question of whether or not there was actual value in the stock. Kahneman goes on to explain the behavior. He theorizes that when faced with a difficult question, we often answer an easier one instead, usually without noticing the substitution. This substitution can be modified by intuition, especially if Herbert Simon's definition of intuition is considered.

Herbert Simon's definition is….

"Intuition is nothing more and nothing less than recognition." . Herbert Simon is another well renowned scientist and is quoted by Kahneman.

Therefore, if the individual has relevant experience and expertise, the thought process will be speeded up and it is likely to result in more appropriate decisions. Even if the decisions are made at speed, if you have encountered the situation before, you can use recognition and thus you are more likely to appear to have made the speedy decision thoughtfully, rationally and devoid of emotion. Since your recognition is based on repeated practice your recognition takes the place of slow thought.

The repeated practice as stated by Simon is related to habits by the fact of repeated practice. Repeated practice will then lead to a decision habit. Conversely, habitual thinking can cloud judgment such as when staff or managers habitually think negatively of certain situations (such as the business planning and budgeting exercises companies generally have to go through). Thus intuition is related to habits; intuition can be developed through practiced and habitual thinking in decision making. I raise this point since most of my writing is about habits and along the habits theme.

What Has Kahneman Got To Do With Management?

Andy Cor

Management Terms

Professor Kahneman, , uses terms such as sunk costs; anchoring, availability and substitution to explain his central thesis of the conflict between thinking fast and thinking slowly and suggests that people are over confident in their judgment. He explores phenomena such as availability bias (using readily available information to answer questions); confirmation bias (where we support our intuitive decision making with selected information that fits that decision) and other biases in our thinking. Professor Kahneman believes that managers and other decision makers could make more optimum decisions by understanding how our brain works.

The Application Scenario

Andy Cor uses a specific scenario to illustrate the underlying principles in understanding how our brain works and the use of Professor Kahneman's principles for management. The application to management of Professor Kahneman's principles of how we think and decision making is explored in the following chapters. Professor Kahneman's key principles are outlined with each principle immediately being followed by an example. So that there is a cohesive, familiar example, Kahneman's key principles are applied to a generic corporate budgeting process throughout the discussion.

The budgeting process is a process that all managers, no matter what the discipline, have to be familiar with. I assume this applies to you, my reader. The easiest scenario to demonstrate the application of Professor Kahneman's principles is to that of a branch manager in a medium sized industrial supplies company and this manager is responsible (among other duties) for constructing a sales budget. It is assumed the branch manager is also responsible for reporting the subsequent actual sales against the budget.

This should be a familiar scenario to most managers either directly or through discussion with those that are directly and extensively involved in the budgeting process. Try to put yourself in that branch manager's shoes as you go through the examples in this book. Otherwise try to relate your own experiences with that of the branch manager and in this way you gain the most benefit from this book. We will start with the key principles first and then go onto the specific areas relevant to managers.

The Key Principles

1. Thinking fast and thinking slow – understand the differences.

Fast thinking is characterized by impulsive, intuitive judgments and is
the more frequent decision making mode. The deeper the
management experience, the more accurate the management decision
will be since the manager will have had the opportunity to practice
and to consider the decisions in the same situation.

Example:

One example of the general application of fast thinking is that of
drills by an athlete, or drills and practice by students. With the drills
come practice and thus the ability to think fast. This is the same
reasoning as to why you, the manager, need your trainees to go
through training courses. Not only do they acquire knowledge, but
they also acquire the experience as to the correct decision to make in
relevant situations.

Conversely, slow thinking is characterized by careful, logical thought. It is of course, much harder work and thus is performed less frequently according to Kahneman. Slow thinking would be necessary when deciding on non-routine type decisions or more complicated decisions you have to make as a manager.

Example:

An example for you in management would be the deep and extensive thinking you have to go through when participating the budgeting and business planning process. You definitely have to think, you have to do your research and sometimes you have to make assumptions. Contrasted with fast thinking where you simply snap out an answer, it is clear to see that slow thinking is harder work than fast thinking.

2. Answering the wrong question

A second key principle discussed by Professor Kahneman is that of answering the wrong question. This refers to the bias toward answering the easier question rather than the right question. This will become clearer to you in the example below. Another aspect of answering the wrong question is that instinct can lead to the wrong decision. Many of the instinctive responses are also due to over confidence according to Professor Kahneman.

Example:

We can illustrate this principle by again using the business planning and budgeting process. Some of the assumptions for the business plan might address the incorrect underlying reasons for some business behaviors. In my experience, this is particularly obvious in sales projections.

For example, we, as senior managers, might ask a branch manager for a reasoned projection for next year's sales. It is significantly easier for the branch manager to answer the question of "what growth would you like to see, say 5% – then add that 5% to last year's sales." The branch manager thus adds about 5% to last year's sale and – voila! There is your answer. Sound familiar to you?

The speedy response could be due to over confidence that growth will come from increasing the sales activity toward the key, volume customers. However, is this really true? In your own experience, can you truly say that you can increase your revenue by simply getting more volume sales from your key customers?

In my experience, this approach inevitably results in having to frequently revise the projections as the year unfolds! I know, I have squirmed in my chair searching for a reasonable answer to support why the sales are not what I said they would be. The reason is that the branch manager is answering the wrong question, the question of desired growth, rather than the question of "…what is a reasonable projection for next year's sales?"

3. Asking the right question

Asking the right question is about finding the correct question to ask. It is generally a challenging question.

"…what is a reasonable projection for next year's sales?"

is more challenging than

" what is 5% growth on last year's sales?".

Clearly, if a branch manager had been accustomed to simply adding a growth percentage to previous periods sales, then, some reorientation is required to get to asking and therefore to answering the right question. This can be termed "prepping" or training the manager. So you need to consider at your next budgeting cycle if you have really been correctly prepped or alternatively, have you sufficiently prepped your own management?

Example:

Let us go back to the business planning and budgeting example in the previous section. The question should rather be something more along the lines of

"Based on your detailed research or knowledge of your key customers what do you see the sales as being for next year? "

This approach would require you as the branch manager to carefully consider the key customers' potential plans. You need to consider their effect on your business through detailed research by you into the local economics and the direction that customer is indicating for his business. Of course, you need to make some deductions, since it is unlikely that a customer is outright going to reveal their strategy and planning details to you! You may be able to get some confirmation or some sort of sign that your deductions are correct, depending on your relationship with that customer.

However, you do need to put in relevant research in preparation for a more accurate and considered answer. While budgeting and business panning is often considered one of the banes of a managers' job, it nevertheless, is a critical activity in preparing for the business going forward. You as the manager need to have some idea of what to expect in the coming year, particularly if a significant customer will be downsizing or expanding and this has an effect on our company's anticipated sales volume to that customer.

Having gathered the data, you should get your sales people to document and analyze the potential effect of each of the major customer's action on your business. It is much easier just to take last year's sales and add a growth percentage – but the decision is incorrect on every level and has its consequences. A research based, considered decision has a strong upside.

During the year, you will be armed with the information to give a reasoned explanation as to why sales might be varying from budgets. This is particularly true if you have a new sales territory to take care of or if you are new to a position. Having the explanations to hand of what was expected to happen with major customers and the expected impact on sales is always very much more useful than having a nebulous 5% growth factor added to the prior period sales. You will look smarter, more prepared and actually appear to be some kind of whizz kid when you apply this process to your next budgeting cycle!

Thus the preparation put into preparing the budget helps you prepare to answer the *right* question, rather than the *easy* question. The monthly reporting of variance against budget will also be more meaningful to you and to the senior executives of your company. You answer the questions regarding the plans and actions of major customers and the effect on sales; nothing more; everything supported against expectation and you will be deemed as highly competent in your job!

Relevance for Managers

4. Significance of priming

Priming and anchoring mean much the same thing in the context of budget setting. It refers to using history to set the stage for the future. In essence it is about setting the scene and suggesting the ultimate outcome.

Example:

Returning to the budgeting scenario, say, you as the manager have been primed with the suggestion that growth should be 5% compared to last year. However, your focus would now be on answering the right question. Nonetheless, now you know that it would be to your advantage not only to answer the right question but to answer it to the extent that you can demonstrate the 5% growth as being achievable or not.

In this way you are likely to continue searching for revenue impacts until the 5% growth on revenue can be explained or supported. The importance of this for senior managers is that to obtain realistic budgeting figures, executives and senior managers need to understand that managers need to be guided both as to the extent of the required growth and the need for considered, slow thought in coming to a thoroughly researched answer. If you do this and recognize the signals for what they are, you will be a more successful manager and you will waste less time and resources by answering the right question to the right depth!

5. The instinct for a coherent story

Another principle discussed by Professor Kahneman that is useful to you as a manager is the instinct we have for a coherent story. While we may prefer rapid responses rather than having to think deeply and extensively before providing a response, we also tend toward providing answers that are geared toward certainty rather than uncertainty. Furthermore, our minds work toward forming a coherent story from the responses. The outcome of this that we may be quick to come to conclusions on certain things and then we become determined to support the conclusions even if there is persuasive evidence indicating a different conclusion. It is important to note that Professor Kahneman points out that logic is not dominant over coherence. Let us clarify what we mean through the use of an example in the budgeting scenario.

Example:

From personal experience, I have observed that managers will give me a quick-fire answer regarding the direction a key customer is taking in that manager's territory. If that specific customer has been in growth mode for the last five years, the manager will have no reason to believe the mode will change.

However, it may be that the company is going to do something different in that territory and the manager has not done the research. The manager has used instinctive answers based on what he already knows. This is the coherence part of the story. Logically, the probability of continued growth is not necessarily a high probability since history is not always a good predictor of the future.

When the revenue figures do not meet budget due to the significant customer taking a different direction, the manager may well justify his answer by indicating the plausibility of his original answer. However, the manager has lost credibility in the eyes of the executive. So what you as the manager need to guard against in your management practices is to consider each customer fully and totally, talk to your customer, don't make assumptions. Your butt is on the line for the answers to the budgeting variance, so do the research and get to the right question and a fully considered documented, answer in the beginning. This will save you embarrassment in the future, believe me!

6. The powerful effect of stereotypes

Here is another dangerous thought process that professor Kahneman discusses in his book that is totally relevant to management. Stereotyping refers to a prejudgment or prejudice regarding people, places and actions. For example, accountants are generally stereotyped as dry and devoid of humor. I am an accountant so I know the stereotyping associated with accountants, and it is true for me – I have no sense of humor.

Example:

We return yet again to our budgeting scenario to illustrate stereotyping and its danger. Within the budgeting it may be that the branch customers are to be grouped into various groups such as current customers, brand new customers and lost customers. By characterizing a customer as lost, for example, stereotypes that customer as not requiring effort, no point in approaching that customer or trying to convert that customer. This is a slippery slope indeed – the stereotyping closes opportunity and leads to poor decisions. So you as the manager need to seriously consider the underlying reasons for the loss. Reasons could be anything from a personality clash to a change in direction. Whatever it is, put in the effort to find out and determine if the customer is worth recovering.

Dismissing the customer outright as lost is potentially a lost source of
quality revenue and is a real negative effect of stereotyping.

7. The Power of first impressions

The phenomenon of the power of first impressions is well known through everything and is closely related to stereotyping.

Example:

The key to understanding the power of first impressions is that associative memory causes us to jump to conclusions. So, for example if we perceive somebody as being aggressive simply because they state the facts without regard to diplomacy, we would be less inclined as managers to forgive judgment errors made by that person.

However, if we perceived somebody as intelligent and thereafter that person stated the facts, we would be forgiving and not label that person as aggressive when stating the facts.   Clearly the order of the impressions are important, first impressions count and once the opinion is formed on that first impression, it becomes difficult to change our views. Every manager needs to understand how to control their thinking so as to make an informed decision both about their staff and about their customers. Every meeting should be as clean a slate as possible and try to be open minded with that person rather than judgmental. Recognize that the first one or two characteristics that stood out at the initial meeting are the ones that are going to dominate your thinking about that person. Additional attributes gained at subsequent meetings tend to be add-ons. not only do you need to guard against your own snap judgments but you do also need to craft your own preferred first impression. If you appear disorganized at first or ill-informed or as having poor product knowledge then that is the image that you are stuck with at every subsequent meeting with that new staff member, executive, or customer or client – make sure it does not happen to you! There is a huge volume more that we could go into as to managing your first impression and then sequencing your subsequent impressions to craft an excellent impression of yourself. This will be in a follow up book within the near future.

Summary: Relevance for Managers

In summary, we all think in two different speeds: fast and slow. Our preference is for faster, more instinctive thinking rather than the slower, more difficult, logical and rational thinking. With the preference toward faster thinking comes bias and therefore mistakes in judgment and it these mistakes that managers must strive to reduce. Through understanding the principles Professor Kahneman discusses and guarding against our natural tendency toward poor decision making, managers can develop a habit of smarter thinking. With smarter thinking, managers are equipped to prepare themselves and their staff for better personal and corporate results.

Thinking Fast and Slow: Revealed – The Surprising Truth about What Kahneman Means for Management

The key areas outlined and applied in Thinking Fast and Slow: Revealed – The Surprising Truth about What Kahneman Means for Management

> The Significance of priming – setting the stage and practicing answering the right question with careful , practiced thought. How to avoid answering the wrong question.

> The instinct for a coherent story: Missing facts are substituted in the fast answer. Coherence is more natural than plausibility.

> The powerful effect of stereotypes and how to stay off the slippery slope of stereotyping.

> The power of first impressions and how to craft the perfect image.

Conclusion

In conclusion, I hope this quick discussion has helped you to understand a bit more about how people think. With this understanding, I am confident that you can use this knowledge to your advantage and to further develop yourself as a person and as a manager. You can see the surprising truth is that the principles discussed by Kahneman, a Nobel Prize winning psychologist, in his book are highly relevant to management!

Thank you for reading this book.

ABOUT THE BOOK AND THE AUTHOR

This book is a practical book, not going too deep, but going deep enough into Professor Kahneman's revelations. The author goes deep enough to give some practical insights into how managers can use Kahneman's principles to avoid making the wrong decisions; and in doing so, how to become better managers.

Books by Andy Cor

Revealed - the Fool Proof Method for Using Gossip to your Advantage in Management

The Power of Habit: The Simple System of How To Reprogram Your Mind For Success

Thinking Fast and Slow: Revealed – The Surprising Truth about What Kahneman Means for Management

Rapid Results from Simple Dumbbell Routines

Why We Get Fat: And What Not To Do About It

Hidden Life of Dogs : A Weekend with Rosie the Beagle

Gardening Jobs for Beginners

Don't Make Me Think: 10 Top Things Guiding Web Usability Design.